Sharyn CRAIG and Pamela MOSTEK

QUILT
challenge
"what if"
ideas for color and design

Martingale®
& COMPANY

Quilt Challenge: "What If" Ideas for Color and Design
© 2009 by Sharyn Craig and Pamela Mostek

Martingale & COMPANY ®

That Patchwork Place®

That Patchwork Place® is an imprint of
Martingale & Company®.

Martingale & Company
20205 144th Ave. NE
Woodinville, WA 98072-8478 USA
www.martingale-pub.com

Printed in China
14 13 12 11 10 09 8 7 6 5 4 3 2 1

Library of Congress Cataloging-in-Publication Data
Library of Congress Control Number: 2009013173

ISBN: 978-1-56477-911-3

CREDITS

President & CEO • Tom Wierzbicki

Editor in Chief • Mary V. Green

Managing Editor • Tina Cook

Technical Editor • Laurie Baker

Copy Editor • Sheila Chapman Ryan

Design Director • Stan Green

Production Manager • Regina Girard

Illustrator • Laurel Strand

Cover & Text Designer • Shelly Garrison

Photographer • Brent Kane

MISSION STATEMENT

Dedicated to providing quality products
and service to inspire creativity.

DEDICATION

To my invaluable seamstress, assistant, and dear friend, Edi Dobbins, who lost her valiant battle with cancer after she completed her work on this book. She added her expert sewing skills to a number of the quilts, and I will forever think of her when I see them.

~Pamela Mostek

ACKNOWLEDGMENTS

Wow! We can't believe we've actually done it. After talking about the idea of writing a book together for years, it's finally a reality. Of course we couldn't have done it alone, and here are a few people to whom we'd like to give special thanks. Without them, the book might not have happened. We would like to thank:

Our husbands, Bob Mostek and George Craig, for their moral, physical, and financial support. Their willingness to eat leftovers so we could quilt made a huge difference to these quilts becoming realities.

All the supportive friends who made the fabulous quilts you see in the book. We couldn't have done them all alone. We really appreciate their willingness to take the challenges and run with them. Included in this list are Margret Reap, Carolyn Smith, Laurine Leeke, Pat Hook, Marnie Santos, Sandy Andersen, Valerie Curtis, Mary Pavlovich, Dee Wills, Nancy Brisack, Carol MacQuarrie, Edi Dobbins, Jean Van Bockel, Retta Wareheim, Gayle Noyce, Pam Kantrud, Louise Hixon, Lynn Johnson, Barbara Hutchins, Carole Shumaik, and Pat Marean. They are fabulous quilt designers, every one!

And then there are all the ladies who did the quilting on so many of these tops. Thank you Ellen Patton, Laurie Daniels, Wendy Knight, Phyllis Reddish, Robin Ruiz, Carol MacQuarrie, and Judi Sample. Without the finishing touch of their expert vision and skill, these quilts would not have had the spirit and soul that you see in these pages. Bless you one and all!

Martingale & Company for taking a chance on our vision. We appreciate the opportunity to bring our ideas to other quilters. You made this journey a joy.

Special thanks from Pam to Bernina for providing her with a fabulous sewing machine. She can attest that it's true—nothing runs like a Bernina!

CONTENTS

How It All Began 6

Take the Challenge 7

Challenge (1) The Color Purple 8

Challenge (2) X Marks the Spot 14

Challenge (3) Churn It Up 22

Challenge (4) Pastel Parts 28

Challenge (5) Black, White, and Red All Over 34

Challenge (6) Neutral Does It 40

Challenge (7) Plaid Garden 48

Challenge (8) Opposites Attract 56

About the Authors 64

HOW IT ALL BEGAN

We are both quilters, teachers, designers, authors…and friends. Although between us we have authored more than 20 books, this is the first book we've written together, and the journey has been exciting, rewarding, and most of all, fun.

Our story began in 2003 when Sharyn was writing her book *Great Sets*. Pam was assigned as the editor. As a team working on the book, we communicated regularly, working out the details.

But that wasn't all. Because of our easy rapport, we also began chatting on a personal level and found we had lots in common: not only our passion for quilting but our devotion to our families. We shared tales of being grandmas, stories of being on the road as quilting teachers, and the loving support of our husbands of 30-plus years. These common interests were more than enough to start a long-distance friendship. We emailed "regular novelettes" over the next few years, filled with shared ideas and answered questions, and generally learned from each other.

Although we both work in the quilting world, our experiences have been different. Sharyn has spent more than 25 years on the road as a dedicated quilting teacher. Pam, on the other hand, began teaching later in her career but has designed fabric and started her own publishing company, Making Lemonade Designs. Between the two of us, if it has anything to do with the world of professional quilting, we've probably done it.

The idea of doing a book together popped up a time or two in our conversations, but it was quickly squelched; we both agreed it was too much of a time commitment. In fact, we kept on saying that until we came up with an idea we couldn't turn down!

The inspiration struck while we were working in Sharyn's sewing room. Pam made a set of Wonky Log Cabin blocks and challenged Sharyn to put her magic to work and see what she could do. Sharyn's specialty! Here was a chance to see just what we could come up with, beginning with Pam's personal style and combining it with Sharyn's passion for putting blocks together.

At that point, we knew we had an idea that had to be shared. What if we gave quilters a block and color assignment and a challenge to develop a quilt in their own personal style? There would be no precise recipes, just guidelines and encouragement to break out of the box and create!

And here are the results. *Quilt Challenge* is an exciting collection of quilts, ideas, and tips, all dedicated to inspiring and challenging each of you to create quilts that are uniquely your own. We both agree; you're going to love the creative journey, as well as the results.

Our best, Pam and Sharyn

Welcome! We're very pleased and excited to bring you this book full of ideas and inspiration for making great quilts. After seeing them all, we hope you'll soon be creating your own fabulous quilts using our color and design ideas.

This book is not only about making quilts; it's also about challenging yourself and your quilting friends, using a basic set of guidelines as a starting point. From there, the sky's the limit as to what fabulous results you can come up with!

Here's how it works. We developed eight different challenges. For each of them, we started with a basic block and a color idea. You'll see the quilts we made, plus we also invited a number of other quilters to take the same challenges, and we've included their quilts as well.

The color assignments will cover a wide range, from soft pastel to black-white-and-red. The blocks, too, are quite different from each other. We've tried to include enough variety so that you will find a challenge idea that excites you. Who knows, maybe you'll opt for a block from one challenge and the color assignment from a different one.

When you've finished the tour of the quilts in our book, you're ready to start creating! Remember, there are no rules for specific quilts. This is your chance to create your own unique quilt. These challenges are a great place to start, but let your own creativity be your guide. And, most importantly, enjoy the process!

setting up a challenge

Whether you're an all-alone quilter living miles from a quilt shop or part of a busy group of quilters, we can all learn from a quilt challenge. It's about pushing ourselves in new directions and fearlessly trying new ideas, not just staying with the same thing we've always done.

Challenges have always been a popular part of quilting. They range from large national challenges to guild and local quilt show challenges, as well as countless small-group challenges. They are all part of the fabric of quilting.

This book is full of challenge ideas. Pick one of them and announce to your group that you'd like them all to be part of the fun. It will take someone to get the ball rolling...and it might as well be you! Even if you're not part of a group, you can still take one of the challenges. Make it your own personal goal to stretch yourself, and we think you'll be pleased with the results.

Here's a little advice: set a time limit for your challenge. It seems many of us work best with a due date! Be realistic with your time frame, but hold yourself accountable to a finish date.

THE COLOR PURPLE

color

Choose one person in your challenge group to select a purple fabric that everyone will use in their quilt. Our suggestion is to select a fabric that has texture and includes different shades of purple but no other colors. With no other colors in the fabric, each quilter in the group will have the free-dom to go any direction in putting together a color scheme. You'll be amazed at just how different all of the quilts will be!

This is the purple fabric we used for our quilt challenge. Can you find it in each of the quilts shown on pages 8–12?

JELLYBEANS ON PARADE by Sharyn Craig

I used the traditional Rail Fence pattern with only two strips per square and made the colors do the work. I wanted them to march across the surface of the quilt, so I worked with lots and lots of different fabrics and kept pushing the color range. I cut 2½" strips of each fabric, and then cut the strips into 4½" rectangles and arranged them on the wall until I was happy with the way the colors connected across the quilt.

block

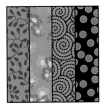

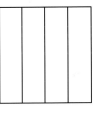

This challenge uses the Rail Fence block—or a variation of it. Traditionally the Rail Fence block is a square made up of equal-width strips of fabric—but there are other possibilities!

GREEN FOR JOSIE by Pamela Mostek

I love working with greens of all shades, and greens are beautiful when paired with purple. Rather than turning the Rail Fence blocks to create angles, I put them together in a diagonal line with a smaller pieced row in between. Because the edges of the quilt were irregular, I trimmed them off to make the quilt rectangular. This quilt is for my granddaughter Josie, who also loves green!

9

BACKGAMMON FOR QUILTERS
by Sharyn Craig

I used teal to contrast with the purple...and not just one teal, but lots of teals and aqua-toned fabrics. I did the same with the purple side of the block. I chose lots of different purple fabrics. I'm much happier using dozens of fabrics than I am using two or three fabrics. The bright pink circles were just a fun addition, chosen to be color accents, but also because when I'd finished the top it reminded me of a backgammon board, so the circles became game pieces.

NO RABBITS ALLOWED
by Margret Reap

Everything about this quilt was spontaneous. The flowers were roughly sketched and fabric was cut out with no pattern. Free-form Rail Fence blocks combined splashes of the purple challenge fabric with a collection of warm country fabrics that I had in my stash. The rabbits were just an impulse idea that I loved for the whimsical feeling they added to the quilt.

BLENDED CULTURES by Carolyn Smith

When Sharyn asked me to make a Rail Fence quilt using the purple fabric, I knew I'd found a home for the *pa ndau* (pronounced "pan dow") I'd had in the drawer for years. The Hmong (pronounced "mung") people came from northern Laos in 1975 after the Vietnam War ended. The women made and sold their traditional embroideries as a source of income for their families. I bought my *pa ndau* for a pittance, and I'm so glad they have finally found a home in my quilt.

MARDI GRAS by Laurine Leeke
....

The purple fabric in this challenge was difficult for me to work with because I normally like to work with softer colors. I chose an accent fabric with purple and several other bright colors. From this fabric I chose my color palette. The curved rail fence was on my list of things to try before being presented with this challenge, so when the design element was the Rail Fence, I knew what direction I would take the quilt.

DESIGN DETAILS

When planning your Rail Fence quilt, start by picking a size for your finished block. It can be square or rectangular—you don't have to use the traditional Rail Fence block. Feel free to bend the rules—and the Rail Fence block—any way you like. Here are a few possibilities to get your creative juices flowing.

The construction method is up to you. You might choose to paper piece, strip piece, or even use templates. The way you create the blocks doesn't matter. By now you probably already have favorite methods for piecing. This is your opportunity to experiment and shine.

There are several traditional arrangements for using Rail Fence blocks, but just like when making the blocks, you don't have to use the traditional approach when laying them out. Anything goes.

sharyn says...

I love the planning phase of making a quilt. I love having a basic assignment, but knowing that it is up to me to interpret it in a personal way. What color or colors do I personally want to use? In getting started I'll often flip through books or magazines looking for color inspiration. My result is often quite different from my inspiration, but at least it's a place to start.

pam says...

How about making your quilt scrappy? Use the purple fabric, but add lots and lots of other colors and fabrics for a totally different look. For a new twist on scrappy, try leaving out one basic color, such as blue or red. This creates an overall look with a distinct personality, even though it's still scrappy. Studying the quilts in the book will give you great color inspiration, no matter what colors you choose.

X MARKS THE SPOT

color

Choose one person in your challenge group to select a multicolored print fabric. Give each person in the challenge a 6" square of this fabric. The challenge is to use only the colors found in this piece of fabric for your entire quilt. You don't have to use all the colors—but no fair adding colors that are not in the swatch!

Choose a fabric with lots of color options. Sharyn stumbled on this Australian print in a quilt shop while on one of her teaching trips and knew the unusual mix of colors would be perfect for the challenge.

BLOOMING Xs by Sharyn Craig

I love creating a pieced frame for my original blocks. In this quilt I pieced triangles to position on each side of the original X blocks. Framing can add so much character to otherwise ordinary blocks and can unify your colors if they aren't cohesive. I alternated my original blocks with more X blocks that have plain black triangles surrounding them. With the framed blocks set on point, it's difficult to figure out how the actual quilt was constructed.

ELEPHANTS ON PARADE by Pamela Mostek

This one is definitely about the fabric. Digging down through my stash, I found this fabulous African fabric that I'd bought who knows when…but the colors were just right for this challenge. I put the blocks together in horizontal rows with marching animals moving across it. For the alternate blocks, I cut up the rows so that different animals were in the blocks, and then made the X blocks with different backgrounds. This one will go to my grandson one of these days!

block

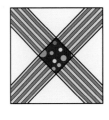

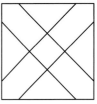

This time you'll use the X block for the basis of your quilt design. You can make the X in your block any size you prefer, from fat to skinny or anywhere in between! Here are a couple of examples; see more examples in "Design Details" on page 20.

15

HUGS AND KISSES by Sharyn Craig

A lot of batiks went into the creation of this quilt. Because the fabrics had less contrast between the values, that meant I had to think carefully about the actual colors. I knew I wouldn't be able to create the pattern through value alone. I wanted some of the blocks to be very, very low contrast and others to be a bit higher. For me, working in low contrast is definitely a stretch. I'm much more comfortable working with high contrast and visually bright colors. I do love this quilt and know I learned a lot from its creation.

CROSSING OVER TO THE ABSTRACT
by Pat Hook

I had this great fabric that reminded me of an abstract painting and never knew what to do with it. Then Sharyn gave me the swatch for the X block and my first thought was how perfect that fabric would be. I combined it with the striped fabric and used black dotted fabric for my X blocks. I had extra X blocks after the quilt center was pieced, so I sliced them in half for my border. I am so happy with how this quilt turned out. If it weren't for the challenge, I might never have figured out how to use that funny fabric.

WACKY Xs by Pat Hook

I had so much fun making the first quilt that I wanted to do another. I looked at my stash and found fabric that I had used for another quilt, and the colors were perfect for this challenge. I had just enough left to make Four Patch blocks. The X block has so many possibilities that I'm already thinking about my next one!

SEW SARI by Marnie Santos

I found a beautiful sari in a resale shop and had to own it. When I realized that it had nearly every color of the challenge fabric swatch in it, it became my fabric of choice for this challenge. The quilt is small because when I cut the flower blocks, all I had left was enough scraps of the sari fabric to make the X blocks, and even one of those is pieced with scraps of the fabric. Even the binding is from the edges of the sari.

BOUQUET by Nancy Brisack

I decided to create an adaptation of a watercolor painted by Charles Rennie Mackintosh (1868–1928) from the Glasgow School of Art. The small flowers around the edges of the quilt were cut from the X blocks. It was definitely a fun challenge to work within the colors of the swatch of fabric.

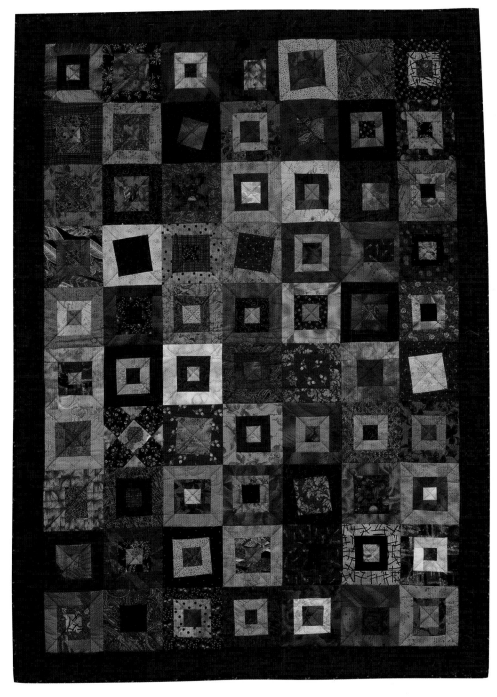

WHERE'S THE X? by Sharyn Craig

By the time I made this quilt, I'd already completed two quilts for this challenge. I made it a personal goal this time to make the quilt fit within the parameters of the challenge but look as different as possible from the others I'd done. I narrowed the color palette dramatically and worked with brown and black with a touch of green and red. In my previous two quilts the brighter colors dominated. Now, look hard to see if you can find the X. It's there, really it is.

DESIGN DETAILS

You can use only the X block or you can combine it with any other block or blocks that you like.

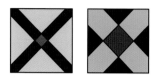

For an easy way to create scrappy X blocks, try these step-by-step instructions. Start with 9" squares. You'll need one square for every block you want to make. These instructions will result in a 6" finished block.

1. With right sides up and values alternated, stack your squares into groups of four to six squares.

2. Enlarge the pattern on page 21 by 133%. If you want to adjust the width of the X in the block, make the adjustment on the copy. Make as many copies of the pattern or adjusted pattern as you have stacks of squares. Roughly cut out the patterns. Using a temporary-bond glue stick, adhere the paper-pattern guide to the right side of the top square in each stack.

3. Using a rotary cutter and ruler, cut on the pattern outer edges to remove the excess fabric.

sharyn says...

The blocks will be trimmed to size after they're pieced together, so you don't have to cut exactly on the outer line. I like to cut out my squares just slightly beyond the line so I have a little bit of extra fabric to work with.

4. Cut on the internal lines through all the fabric layers, again using your rotary cutter and ruler. Remove the paper guide pieces from the top layer. Reassemble one pattern to use as a reference for scrambling the pieces.

5. Referring to the reassembled pattern or the pattern in the book, scramble the pieces in each stack. The numbers on the pattern will help you scramble the pieces in each section. Each number tells you how many pieces of fabric to take from the top of each individual section and move to the bottom of that same section. For instance, there is a 2 on the center square. Take the top two pieces of fabric in that section and move them to the bottom of that section. Repeat for each section in each stack, making sure to move the exact number it tells you to.

6. Sew the blocks together as shown.

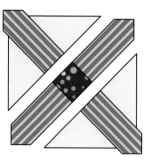

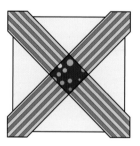

7. After the blocks are sewn, trim them to 6½" square, keeping the X centered.

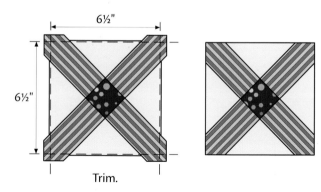

Trim.

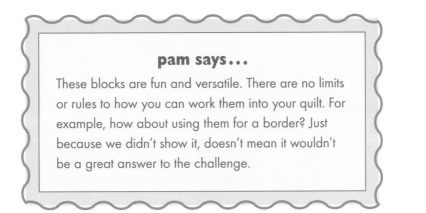

pam says...

These blocks are fun and versatile. There are no limits or rules to how you can work them into your quilt. For example, how about using them for a border? Just because we didn't show it, doesn't mean it wouldn't be a great answer to the challenge.

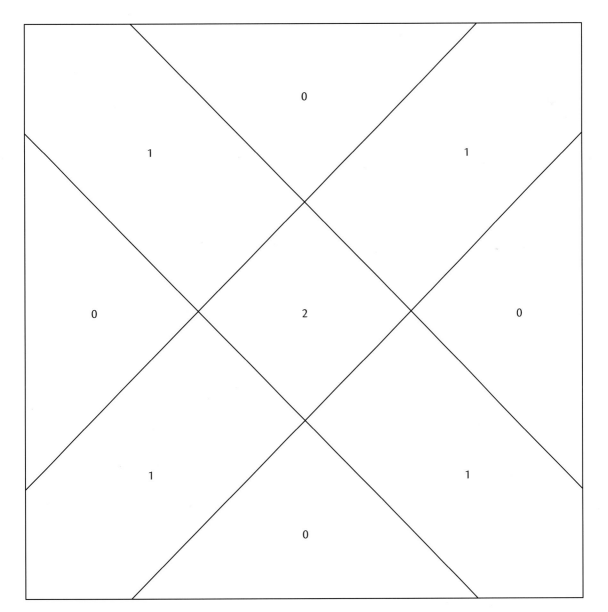

Enlarge pattern 133%.

CHURN IT UP

color

This time we want you to use only red fabrics and light fabrics in your blocks. The light fabrics can be whites or creams. Once your blocks are made, you can add any color or colors you like, but not in the original blocks.

CHURNING CHOCOLATE by Sharyn Craig

I decided to make a quilt using only blocks with red backgrounds. I wanted to avoid the obvious color schemes that go with red and white, which made me think of brown. I wanted the quilt to be warm, strong, and cozy feeling. Starting with adjectives like this often helps give me a sense of direction. Otherwise it can be a little overwhelming to make a decision about which direction to go.

CHURN DASH IN PROVENCE by Pamela Mostek

When Sharyn gave me this set of red-and-light blocks, the first thing I did was cut them into pieces…just for a little variety. Then I sewed them back together with multicolored strips in various widths between the crooked pieces. I combined them with bright prints I had purchased in Provence, France, which gave the entire quilt a bright, cheerful, and a little bit wonky look.

block

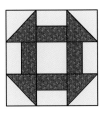

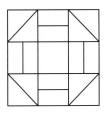

The Churn Dash has always been one of our favorite blocks. It's definitely a classic block that has been around for generations. We hope you'll have as much fun making the blocks as we did.

23

PASTEL CHURN by Sharyn Craig

My personal goal here was to use the very obviously red-and-light blocks to make a pastel quilt. There's no arguing that the red is there, but overall what the viewer sees and feels is a very soft, romantic, spring-like quilt. I used a pieced chain sashing as a way of making the viewer's eye travel around the quilt.

RED SQUARE by Sharyn Craig

To make a quilt that is just red and light is a huge challenge to someone that loves color as much as I do. This time, that is exactly what I knew I had to do. I'm only going to grow and learn as a quilter if I do things that aren't always easy.

THE SURVIVOR by Margret Reap

In October 2003, as a wildfire threatened our home, we had to make some swift decisions about our belongings. While my husband rescued his gun collection, my thoughts were on my quilts. My Bernina, several quilts, and a box of exchange blocks and related fabrics came with me. Our home was lost in the fire, but that box of "parts" became an important step in my return to normalcy. I used the rescued blocks and fabrics in this quilt.

ROASTED CHICKEN by Margret Reap

The day after losing our home in that terrible wildfire, we surveyed the rubble and found all our chickens had survived. This quilt is a celebration of those chickens. The chicken fabric was an impulse purchase; the wonderful, bright fabrics came from friends; and the Churn Dash blocks were among items taken when we evacuated our home. I love this quilt. It makes me smile and reminds me that even the darkest cloud has a silver lining.

25

RUNNING RED by Laurine Leeke

I was a part of the Churn Dash block challenge and my personal color challenge was to add green and orange to my red-and-white blocks. I named the quilt "Running Red" because one of the reds ran when washed! I enjoy the quilt for all the happy memories it brings from our group project.

LADY LIBERTY by Carolyn Smith

When I saw the border fabric, I had to have it—I just didn't have anything to use it for at the time. As soon as I saw the Churn Dash blocks from our group exchange, I knew it was fate. I picked up the blue from the border and used it in the corners of the blocks. Without the border fabric, I never would have thought of that, and look what a spark that blue gives the quilt.

26

DESIGN DETAILS

The fun part here is not only creating the red-and-white Churn Dash blocks but also choosing a color scheme for the rest of the quilt. You'll be amazed at how you can transform the entire look of the quilt depending on the other colors you use. Just because the blocks are red and white doesn't mean you have to have a red-and-white quilt when you're finished. And they all don't have to be the same size either. Use the chart below to make a variety of block sizes to use in your quilt, like Sharyn did with the Variable Star blocks in "Nonfat Mocha" on page 40.

The Churn Dash blocks we used for the challenge finished to 6"; however, on the following chart you will find dimensions to vary the size if you prefer.

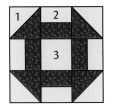

Finished Block Size	Piece 1	Piece 2	Piece 3
6"	2⅞" ◻	1½" x 2½"	2½" x 2½"
7½"	3⅜" ◻	1¾" x 3"	3" x 3"
9"	3⅞" ◻	2" x 3½"	3½" x 3½"
12"	4⅞" ◻	2½" x 4½"	4½" x 4½"
◻ Cut once diagonally from corner to corner.			

sharyn says...

The problem with a two-color quilt that has a high contrast in color value (red and white for example) is that it can be so intense that the quilt becomes hard to look at. The secret is to *not* end up using the dark value (red in this case) in 50% of the quilt and the light value (white in this case) in the other 50%. You need more of one value than the other to give the eye a resting spot. It doesn't make any difference which direction you go, dark or light, but choose one.

pam and sharyn say...

All the blocks for the quilts shown were made by the same group of quilters and traded. By doing this we were guaranteed that the intensity and values of the reds would be different, as would the clarity of the lights. We did stipulate that we each had to make some of our blocks with light backgrounds and some with red backgrounds. This creates a positive and negative effect. If you're thinking about a group challenge we definitely recommend this one. It's a simple block, simple color assignment, not many decisions to make, and obviously this block provides great potential.

PASTEL PARTS

color

Soft and subtle pastels are the color assignment for this challenge. You choose the colors—just keep the shades light in tone. Does that mean you can only use pastel colors in the rest of the quilt? Not necessarily— you can be creative here. Once the blocks are made and it's time to put them together into a quilt, you can add any colors you like.

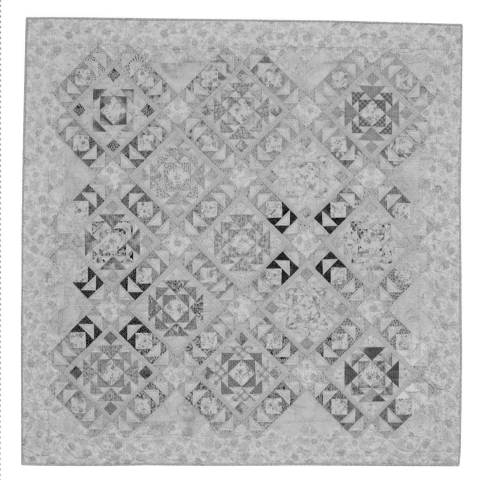

CROSSING GUARD by Sharyn Craig

I frequently look at blocks like the ones used for the challenge and imagine them as parts of bigger blocks. So, when it was time for me to take this challenge, that's exactly what I did. I liked the combination of using the two blocks in one block. I also used strips of flying-geese units as the sashing. I love the secondary star image that emerges where the sashing intersects. I used bright pastel colors for this quilt.

PINK SORBET by Pamela Mostek

Any color combination with low contrast becomes one of my favorites! I enjoy using just enough contrast to make it interesting while keeping the overall look subtle. For this challenge, I kept my colors all quite light; however, I used slightly darker shades for the larger triangle in the B blocks. When I put four of these blocks together to make the larger block, a secondary triangle pattern of the darker shades emerged. Block A became the softer background pattern.

blocks

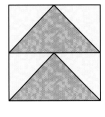

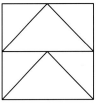

Block A

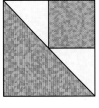

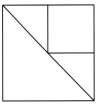

Block B

This time you have two blocks to work with, A and B. You can combine them into a larger block or use them separately. See "Design Details" on page 33 for more information. The blocks our challenge participants used to create their quilts measured 3" finished.

SPRING BLOOM by Pam Kantrud

When I started this challenge I had nothing in my house that was remotely pastel, so I decided I would do something that looked like Easter with the blocks. I also wanted to do some machine appliqué, so I combined that with my pastel blocks. I hang the quilt in the spring to brighten up the living room and dining room.

TRANQUIL POND by Louise Hixon

The idea for this quilt came from an illustration of Chinese carp. I drew the fish and appliquéd them to the green-and-blue fabric, and then used the pastel blocks to frame the fish. I did free-motion embroidery for the water lilies.

PLAYFUL PASTEL PARTS
by Carole Shumaik

Once I had the fabric chosen for the pastel blocks, I decided to use a large-scale floral print from my fabric stash as a way to blend darker and lighter values into the overall design. I thought it would be fun to see if I could make this quilt without purchasing any new fabric. Having to work from what I already had in the house was an extra challenge.

BUTTERFLY GARDEN
by Pat Marean

I was definitely challenged to try something new with this assignment because I am more inclined to work with bright colors. I used a modified vertical bar setting; I have always liked the orderly, structured look of that type of setting. I inserted two columns of flying geese. Next I incorporated a somewhat darker green fabric with trees into the border area to help frame and contain the softer central area.

31

COTTON CANDY by Lynn Johnson

The inspiration for the setting of this quilt came from a photo of a quilt I saw years ago in *Quilter's Newsletter Magazine*. The original had some pastel Dresden Plate blocks. The Dresden Plate pattern has always been a favorite of mine, so I was excited to start this challenge. I combined the Dresden Plate blocks with my pastel blocks.

sharyn says...

To get started on "Crossing Guard" (page 28), I pulled lots of fabric in the pastel shades I'd envisioned. I selected one constant fabric for the background in all the units. Next, I cut enough for four of each block per color choice. I made blocks over a several week period. Then I impulsively selected A blocks to go with B blocks. I didn't worry about if they matched or not.

DESIGN DETAILS

You must use both blocks, but how you put them together is up to you. Maybe you'll combine them to create a larger block, or use them in the border, or integrate them with other blocks or parts of blocks. Here's a chance to put your imagination to work!

Check the chart below for the sizes to cut each of the pieces in the blocks for a 3" finished block. Of course, you can make your blocks any size you want, but this will get you started.

We know there are many methods for creating the flying-geese units used in block A. Any method will work as long as it gives you the result you're after!

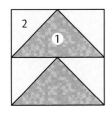

BLOCK A—finished size 3"	
Piece	Size to Cut
1	4¼" x 4¼" ⊠ (enough for 2 blocks)
2	2⅜" x 2⅜" ◳
◳ Cut once diagonally from corner to corner.	
⊠ Cut twice diagonally from corner to corner.	

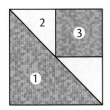

BLOCK B—finished size 3"	
Piece	Size to Cut
1	3⅞" x 3⅞" ◳
2	2⅜" x 2⅜" ◳
3	2" x 2"
◳ Cut once diagonally from corner to corner.	

pam says...

The border that I used for "Pink Sorbet" on page 29 is a great way to finish the quilt. I call it my Blended Borders technique, and I use *broderie perse* appliqué shapes cut from the border fabric, either raw-edged or traditional, positioned on the border seam to blend the quilt center with the border. I don't try to cover the entire seam...just strategically place enough of them to create the blend.

I don't use fusible web to secure them in place. I do, however, use a lot of pins to hold them where I want them until I stitch them down in the quilting stage. My personal favorite is the raw-edged technique because it creates an interesting texture around the shapes.

33

BLACK, WHITE, AND RED ALL OVER

color

The old riddle by the same name was our inspiration here: "What's black and white and read all over?" (Answer: a newspaper.) The bottom line is that you must use black and white with only one other color in your entire quilt. We used red for that color, as did most of the challenge participants. If you prefer, you can substitute another color for red (see "The Blues Sisters" on page 38). Of course, you can use lots of different fabrics in each color, and they can be lots of different tints, values, or shades. Remember, the goal is to work within the challenge rules, not how you can break those rules!

GOOD AND PLENTY by Sharyn Craig

I framed my Nine Patches, turning them into a pieced star-like block. I either made white stars with black backgrounds or black stars with white backgrounds. Next, I made Logs Plus blocks (one of my original designs), using the bright pinks for the triangles that divide these blocks diagonally. I arranged them in the traditional Fields and Furrows pattern, and the stars appear to float on the surface. I used a flowered print fabric (designed by coauthor Pam) to create the *broderie perse* appliquéd border.

block

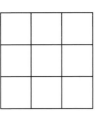

You must use a basic Nine Patch block somewhere in your quilt. That means a square made up of nine smaller squares. You can do anything you like with this basic Nine Patch. Have fun with it!

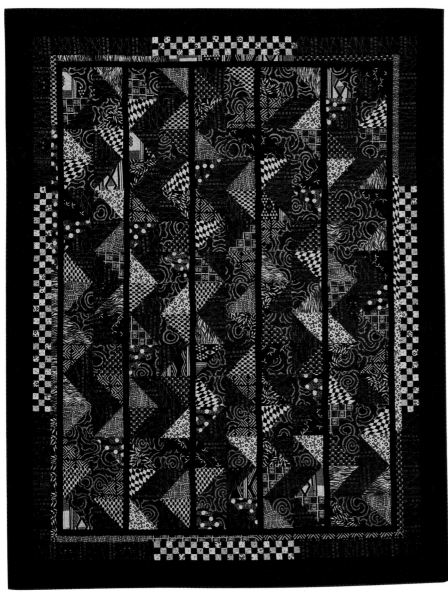

JUNGLE JAZZ by Pamela Mostek

Lurking at the bottom of my fabric stash was a great collection of black-and-white African prints. I even found some red ones in the mix. They were perfect for this challenge. Because the prints were so bold and dramatic, I concentrated on a simple zigzag pattern that showed off the fabrics. Can you find my Nine Patch blocks? They're in the border!

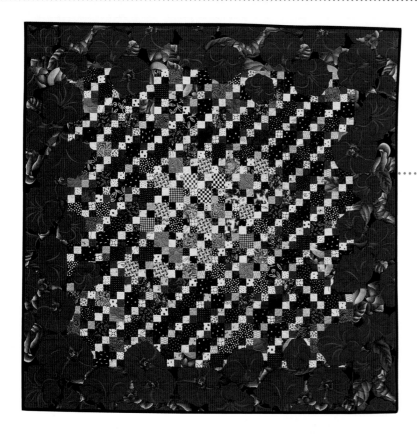

PATTI'S QUILT by Pamela Mostek

The flowers in this print were too gorgeous to cut up so I used them in the border and appliquéd some on the border seam using my Blended Border technique. For the quilt center, I used repeating Nine Patch blocks; however, the ones in the middle are all a lighter shade. This creates a feeling of depth and adds interest to the overall design. For more information on this border technique, refer to page 33.

ANGEL DUST by Edi Dobbins

Edi used an asymmetrical arrangement of Nine Patch blocks to create this simple but striking quilt. The combination of small and large scale in her black-and-white prints creates a lively, blended look. Thanks to Anna Turner and Carol MacQuarrie for helping me finish it according to Edi's vision.

POPPIES by Laurine Leeke

Gardening is a second passion for me—quilting first; then gardening. I took photographs of the red poppies from my garden and enlarged them. I decided to make the flowers a bit more abstract for this quilt, mostly to simplify the image. The iron rails are from my gazebo. This quilt was a whole new style for me and I really enjoyed the process.

OUTSIDE THE BOX
by Laurine Leeke

This quilt came from a Nine Patch and Diagonal Cross class I took from Carolyn Smith. I was not happy with the quilt top when it was done. When Sharyn and Pam suggested this challenge, I thought it might be fun to use the top as a foundation for the "red," thus saving the top. This is the end result and I really am glad they challenged me to step outside the box.

THE BLUES SISTERS
by Barbara Hutchins

Having recently exchanged blue blocks with two different small quilt groups that I belong to, this challenge seemed the perfect opportunity to do something fun with the blocks. It took quite a bit of playing and auditioning fabrics on my flannel design wall before I was satisfied, but I love the end result. I'm so glad Sharyn and Pam invited me to participate.

DESIGN DETAILS

If you prefer, you can substitute another color instead of using red. Of course, you can use many different fabrics for each color, and they can be many different tints, values, or shades. Remember, the goal is to work within the challenge rules, not how you can break those rules!

The blocks can be framed with other piecing. They might become a base for appliqué. You might opt to make an entire quilt of simple squares. The interpretation is totally up to you. With an easy block and an uncomplicated color scheme, this is a great challenge for anywhere from one to one hundred quilters!

Who says a Nine Patch has to have nine equal-sized squares? We didn't tell you that! You can make those nine squares in the block different sizes or the same size. It's a great chance to give a new twist to a favorite old block. The Nine Patches could be alternating blocks to another focus block. Perhaps you'll use the Nine Patches in the border only. The choice is yours. Here are a few Nine Patch possibilities. Have fun with them!

pam says...

Looking for drama? There's nothing more dramatic in a quilt, or any other creative project, than black and white. It always catches the viewer's eye...and maybe the judge's if you're into entering contests with your quilts. Add a ravishing red fabric and you have the perfect formula for a powerful quilt.

sharyn says...

One of the greatest compliments I received about "Good and Plenty" on page 34 came from Pam, who emailed right away after seeing the photo. "Gosh, now you're making quilts that look like mine." Because I admire Pam's quilts so much, and look up to her artistic expertise, I felt really good about her reaction. Understand, it wouldn't have mattered to me whether she liked it or not. I loved it, and that is absolutely the most important thing I keep in mind when making a quilt.

NEUTRAL DOES IT

color

Neutral is *not* a synonym for boring! Your challenge is to make an interesting quilt using neutral fabrics. What is neutral? It can be whites, blacks, grays, tans, khakis, taupes, etc. You can even use a tiny touch of color, as long as that color doesn't play center stage. You can use a narrow range of values or expand the range.

NONFAT MOCHA by Sharyn Craig

Creating quilts that need to be pieced together like jigsaw puzzles can be a fun challenge. On page 47 you'll get some hints on how to start designing a quilt like this. For this quilt I used only Variable Star blocks but in several different sizes. A recent fabric acquisition came at the perfect time. The mocha-like colors satisfied my urge to head to the nearest coffee bar.

SUPERSTARS by Pamela Mostek

Not only did I use a range of taupe colors for this quilt, I also used a variety of different types of fabrics. In the mix are metallics, dupioni silks, fabrics with mysterious fiber content, as well as commercial cotton prints. I used to call myself a cotton snob, but now, anything goes! If I like the color, in it goes! Rather than using many smaller Variable Star blocks, I made only four large ones in order to showcase the large neutral floral prints.

block

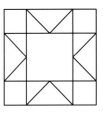

The traditional Variable Star block is your design element this time. Cutting dimensions for various finished block sizes are given on page 46. You don't have to limit yourself to these sizes—we've just given them to you to get you started.

LEFTOVER PLUS SIX by Laurine Leeke

I had been collecting neutral blocks over the years. For the challenge presented by Sharyn and Pam, I made six of the Variable Star blocks to go with the blocks I already had. I love this quilt because I found a home for single blocks that were given to me by friends over the past few years. It's such fun when not only do I get to participate in a challenge, but at the same time I finish a project started years earlier.

DON'T GIVE UP TAUPE by Mary Pavlovich

I love scrap quilts, so using a limited color palette was definitely a challenge. The catalyst came from a collection of taupe fabrics I had purchased at a recent quilt show. Next, I went looking through my stash and came up with several more taupe-based fabrics I could use for this quilt. I loved the challenge, and even more important, I love the finished quilt!

SHOOTING STARS by Carol MacQuarrie

I was very excited to do this challenge because it would give me a chance to create a quilt that would highlight my long-arm quilting. A neutral color scheme is the perfect canvas for that. I love quilting Pam's quilts, but they're usually very colorful and active, and the quilting is secondary. On this one, the quilting is the star of the show!

consider the options

Here's the challenge with a twist—high-contrast appliqués.

VARIABLE TRELLIS by Gayle Noyce

Lately I have been working mainly in batiks, and it was challenging to find neutral batiks to give me enough variety to make a scrappy look. Because I work primarily with bright batiks, the soft shades of gray, green, gold, and blue that I chose were neutrals to me! I set the Variable Star blocks on point and sashed them with a darker brown, which looks like a trellis. I added a flowering appliquéd vine and purchased silk flowers to finish the trellis effect and add a different twist to the challenge.

DESIGN DETAILS

You can make all your blocks the same size or vary the sizes. Sometimes it's fun to make one size block for the body of the quilt and another size for the border. Or perhaps you'll make 8" Variable Star blocks for the focus blocks, with smaller ones for cornerstones in the sashing. We don't want to give you too many ideas because we want you to play with the possibilities yourself. Feel free to mix the Variable Star blocks with other blocks as well.

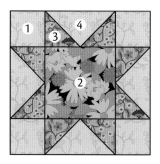

Finished Block Size	Piece 1	Piece 2	Piece 3	Piece 4
6"	2" x 2"	3½" x 3½"	2⅜" x 2⅜" ◺	4¼" x 4¼" ⊠
7½"	2⅜" x 2⅜"	4¼" x 4¼"	2¾" x 2¾" ◺	5" x 5" ⊠
8"	2½" x 2½"	4½" x 4½"	2⅞" x 2⅞" ◺	5¼" x 5¼" ⊠
9"	2¾" x 2¾"	5" x 5"	3⅛" x 3⅛" ◺	5¾" x 5¾" ⊠
12"	3½" x 3½"	6½" x 6½"	3⅞" x 3⅞" ◺	7¼" x 7¼" ⊠
◺ Cut once diagonally from corner to corner.				
⊠ Cut twice diagonally from corner to corner.				

block party

Ever wonder how to make a quilt with lots of different-sized blocks, like Sharyn's "Nonfat Mocha" on page 40? The secret is to start with four-squares-to-the-inch graph paper.

Start in a corner and draw different-sized squares. You can make the squares 4 x 4, 5 x 5, 6 x 6, etc. In doing this you'll occasionally have space gaps where the blocks don't fit snugly together. Not to worry! These become small pieced units. The units can be simple squares, pieced squares, strips, anything.

Once you've drawn your map as large as you want, with as many blocks as you want, then decide what size each of the blocks will be. You can assign any measurement to the squares on the graph paper. The easiest is to assume each square is 1". If that's the case, then a 4 x 4 block is a 4" square, a 6 x 6 block is a 6" square, and so on. Sharyn used a 1½" measurement for the grid shown below. For her quilt she made 6", 7½", 9", and 12" blocks.

sharyn says...

My personal favorite formula is to make each graph paper square equal to 1½". There's something almost magical about what happens when the assigned measurement is 1½". As long as you're working with blocks that have four equal divisions in them, as our Variable Star block does, then you can assign any unit of measurement to each of the graph paper grids and you'll always come out with nice numbers that you can cut without using templates.

If you choose a block that has three equal divisions across it (commonly referred to as a Nine Patch), then it becomes more challenging, *unless* you've used 1½" as your assigned measurement to each graph paper size. For some reason, which I've yet to totally understand, when you do this type of quilt design and assign 1½" per square, you can make any Four Patch or any Nine Patch block and you'll come up with nice numbers for template-free cutting. Try working it out for yourself and you'll see!

PLAID GARDEN

color

The assignment in this challenge is not so much about the specific color, but the patterns in those colors. You'll be using plaids and floral prints, but the colors are up to you. You can stretch your definition of plaid to include checks and stripes if you prefer. The florals can be any scale.

CINNABAR by Sharyn Craig

Positive and negative blocks alternate in this quilt to create interlocking circles. The blocks are set on point, making a softer transition into the border fabric. Using the same bold floral in the blocks, setting triangles, and border is a fun way to focus on the fabric.

TULIPS AT MIDNIGHT by Pamela Mostek

A large-scale home-decor print with vibrant red tulips was the inspiration for my quilt. I combined it with dozens of homespun-looking plaids of all colors, which created an overall dark, dramatic look. For a finishing touch, the scalloped borders repeated the circular effect of the block. This is one of my favorites!

block

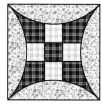

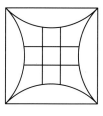

The Glorified Nine Patch is a traditional block that was particularly popular in the 1930s and '40s. Combining the gentle curves of the block with plaids and florals creates very interesting designs in your quilt. You'll find the patterns needed to make the block templates on pages 54 and 55.

49

ROMANCING THE PLAID by Laurine Leeke

I combined a soft, pale green floral with the soft reds of the plaids. I am very pleased with the results, which create a kind of muted effect. I carried the arc shape out into the setting triangles of the eight on-point blocks to finish the circles.

SUNNY GARDEN by Sharyn Craig

I searched a long time for this warm yellow floral with the red roses. As soon as I saw it I knew it was perfect for my kitchen. The black-and-white checkerboard frame around each block punched the blocks up just enough to draw your eye around the quilt. I always want the viewer's eye entertained when looking at my quilts, and this one definitely does that.

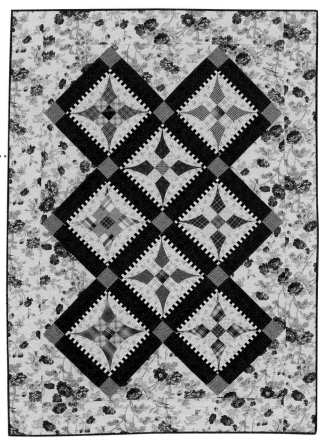

FLOWER FIELDS by Marnie Santos

Finding the right fabric was a challenge, but I enjoyed the hunt almost as much as making the quilt! The idea for the final touch, appliquéing on the flowers, came later and wasn't part of my original plan. When the body of the quilt was done and I stood back and looked at it, a small voice told me to add the three flowers. I'm glad I listened!

PICCADILLY PAISLEY
by Jean Van Bockel

I love doing appliqué, so I made a medallion quilt with an appliquéd Basket block as the center. I found a wonderful paisley fabric that picked up the colors in the appliqués, and then continued to add bright plaid and floral fabrics to the mix. I used the Glorified Nine Patch block for the outside pieced border and created a scalloped effect with the placement of the purple and green fabrics.

RHUBARB PIE
by Retta Wareheim

I was thrilled to be asked to make a quilt for the book—until I got the guidelines. Florals! I never work with florals. I love plaids, but the mix sounded horrifying! I happened to have a few floral fat quarters in my stash that someone had given me, so that's what I used because I started the quilt at 11:00 p.m. when no quilt shop was open. I love using templates, though, so I went to work. I'm very pleased with the results—florals and all. It was a great challenge for me and really tested my color skills.

consider the options

Here's the challenge with a twist—a different block.

SUNNY AND WARM WITH A CHANCE OF SHOWERS by Dee Wills

The block I used is called Sunny Lanes. I chose it because I like the movement and action created by the diagonal line in the block. I found the floral prints and plaids to be a real challenge because they were each so strong. By cutting them into small pieces I was able to control the energy they individually created. Everything started with the great watermelon-colored floral. All the other fabrics were picked to go with it.

DESIGN DETAILS

The Glorified Nine Patch block is a great stand-alone block, but it can also be combined with other blocks. When the pattern was first popular it wasn't made as individual blocks. Instead it was constructed more like a Double Wedding Ring quilt in a continuous allover design. Not only is it easier to piece as individual blocks, but it also totally opens up the setting options when working with these blocks.

Don't be afraid of the T word: templates! They take the math out of the cutting. Just lay the template on the fabric and cut around it with a rotary cutter. Sew the pieces together and...voilà...it's a block! If your templates are accurate, it simplifies your piecing because you know the pieces will all fit together nicely.

sharyn and pam say...

Sewing curves is no more difficult than sewing straight lines. Use a minimum of pins (we suggest no more than three per curved edge), keep the edges together with your fingers, sew slowly, and ease to fit. A slightly longer stitch length will also help when sewing the curves.

template ordering information

To order a set of templates for the 9" Glorified Nine Patch block, contact Sharyn Craig at 619-440-2530, or sharyncraig@cox.net. The templates are $12.50, which includes postage, handling, and detailed instructions.

To make the blocks, use the patterns below and at right to make templates from template plastic, lightweight cardboard, or cardstock; or use premade acrylic templates (see below for information on ordering acrylic Glorified Nine Patch templates). Use the templates to cut out one of piece 1 and four *each* of pieces 2, 3, and 4 from the desired fabrics. Assemble pieces 1–3 into three horizontal rows, and then add piece 4 to each side, adding opposite sides first.

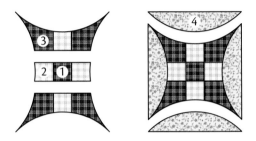

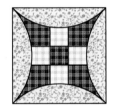

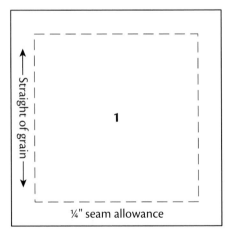

Straight of grain

1

¼" seam allowance

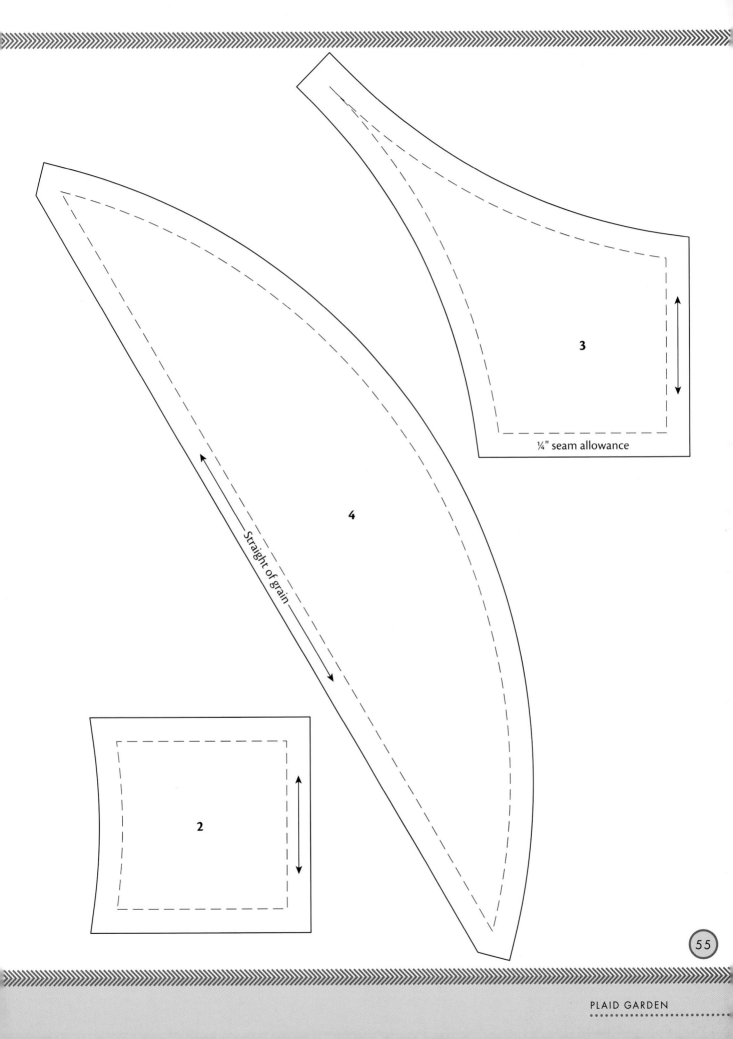

3

¼" seam allowance

4

Straight of grain

2

OPPOSITES ATTRACT

color

This one doesn't have a precise color assignment. Instead we want you to focus on types of fabrics by combining batik and/or hand-dyed fabrics with vintage-looking prints. Most of the quilts pictured here used fabrics inspired by the 1800s, but you can select any past era of design that appeals to you. Like we said, opposites attract!

TEQUILA SUNRISE by Sharyn Craig

"I have a challenge for you, oh Queen of Sets," were the very words that Pam emailed me prior to coming for a visit. She brought a set of the Wonky Log Cabin blocks made in the vintage and batik fabrics. I think she thought she'd have me stumped as to what to do with them. But oh no, not in the least. Of all the challenges, I honestly think this was my favorite. It was extremely out of my comfort zone, but so stimulating!

RASPBERRY SALSA by Pamela Mostek

Every once in a while I make a quilt I absolutely *love*... and this is one of them! Definitely the vividly colored batiks dominate in this quilt. I grouped them in color areas and assembled the blocks side by side. The vintage-looking prints are in there but they aren't as obvious. Still, they are a fabulous complement to the more exotic, vivid batiks. I made it to fit my dining room table and love looking at it there.

block

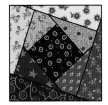

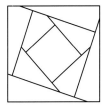

The block format we selected is the Wonky Log Cabin. Because this is the eighth challenge, we're going to be a bit looser with this one. If you'd rather work with a different block, then fine, go for it. We love this Wonky Log Cabin and found it to be very versatile. It's truly the fabric combination that will make this challenge special and unique.

NOW AND THEN by Sharyn Craig

My personal challenge with these Wonky Log Cabin blocks was to make a quilt that looked neither artsy nor vintage, but instead contemporary. I was very pleased with the final results. The quilt lived up to both my goal and my expectations.

CINNAMON SPICE by Pamela Mostek

I took the opposite approach from "Raspberry Salsa" (page 57) here, with the vintage-looking fabrics stealing the show. I found a fabulous, large-scale reproduction print that I used as a background for the blocks and loved the effect it created. I used a smaller Wonky Log Cabin block for the pieced border. For a finishing touch, I appliquéd the floating squares here and there in the background to break up the space a little.

58

THIS ONE'S FOR PAM by Sharyn Craig

"Tequila Sunrise" looked artsy; "Now and Then" turned out contemporary. Let's see if I can make one that feels more like an 1850s quilt. This meant that I had to push the vintage-looking fabrics and the colors to take on that effect. I took the quilt with me when visiting Pam, and she loved it. And darned if it didn't look like it was custom-made for her living room, so now that's where it lives.

A LITTLE BIT COUNTRY, A LITTLE BIT ROCK 'N' ROLL by Sandy Andersen

I've always loved reproduction fabrics and I've always enjoyed batiks…but *together*? You've got to be kidding, was my first thought. I've never been one to run from a challenge, so I decided to embrace this head-on. Certainly since I like both kinds of fabrics there has to be some way to combine them into one quilt that I would also like. I hit many roadblocks along the way, but I absolutely love the final result and am so glad I decided to try this challenge.

consider the options

Here's the challenge with a twist—the Northwind block.

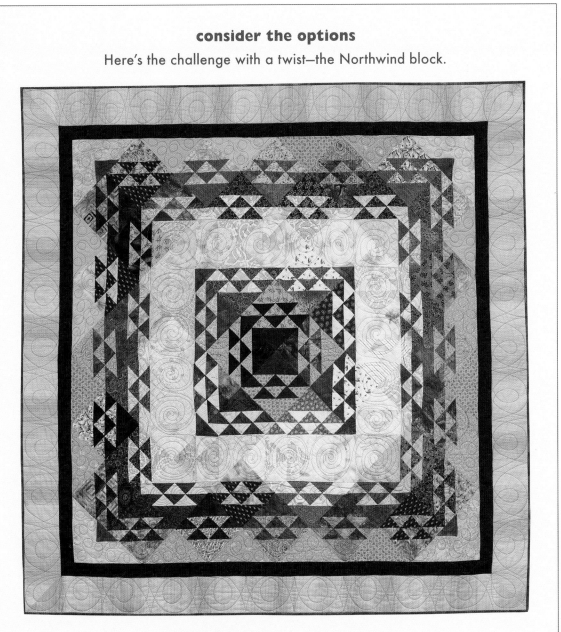

ANTIQUE BATIQUE by Marnie Santos

When I started quilting in the late 1980s, the first class I took was a Northwind class taught by Sharyn Craig. (Little did I know!) I have loved that particular block ever since and this quilt is my tenth Northwind quilt. It turned out looking very antique to my eye, thus the name. I mixed the fabrics in the blocks—batiks with reproductions, all reproductions, and all batiks—and used colors ranging from beige to brown.

consider the options

Here's the challenge with a twist—the Windblown Square block.

WONKY DIDN'T WORK by Valerie Curtis

When I was asked to participate in this challenge, I wondered how in the world I'd be able to combine Civil War prints with batiks. I decided to forget about the fabrics and concentrate on value and color. I used the Windblown Square block. The challenge opened my eyes about combining opposite types of fabrics. The title came about when, after many unsuccessful attempts to use the Wonky Log Cabin blocks as a border, I just couldn't force that square peg into that round hole!

DESIGN DETAILS

This block is a traditional Log Cabin block with a twist. The results will be skewed, but it's still the Log Cabin concept because you're building around a square. To make the blocks:

1. Select the size of your center square and the width of the strips you will sew around it. Most of our quilts began with a 3½" center square. The strips we sewed onto the square were 2½" wide.

2. Sew a round of strips onto the center square.

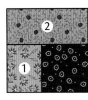 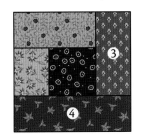

3. Place a 5½" square ruler at an angle over the step 2 unit and trim around it.

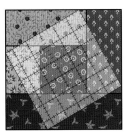 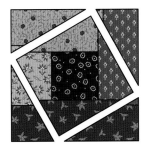

4. Add a second round of strips to the trimmed unit, and then repeat step 3 to trim the unit with a 7½" square ruler.

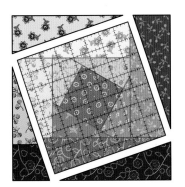

5. Add one more round of strips and trim the unit with a 9½" square ruler.

pamela mostek

Pam's quilts can often be recognized by their blended colors and big bold prints. For her, it's all about the fabric! It's no wonder "fabric designer" is one of the hats she wears in the quilting industry. She is also the owner and designer for her own publishing company, Making Lemonade Designs, and the author of a number of other quilting books and magazine articles. She is also a nationally recognized teacher in the quilting world. She loves creating art quilts, many of which have been included in national shows and exhibits.

Pam lives in Cheney, Washington, with her husband, Bob. She spends any spare time enjoying her four grandchildren and playing in her garden.

sharyn craig

For Sharyn, it's the "what if?" phrase that motivates her as a quiltmaker. She loves playing with blocks and color, with problem solving and innovative settings being her forte. Her love of quilting is definitely matched by the need to share that knowledge with other quilters, which she's been able to do as a national and international teacher since the early 1980s.

Sharyn has authored a number of books and magazine articles. In 1985 *The Professional Quilter* magazine named her their first Quilt Teacher of the Year. In 2004 she was named as one of the top 24 finalists for the All American Quilters award sponsored by the American Quilters Society.

Sharyn lives in El Cajon, California, with her husband, George. She loves being a wife, mother, and grandmother.